DAYS IN DEVONPORT
Part III

Gerald W. Barker

The Final Tram, 29th September, 1945

The final tram from Old Town Street via Peverell corner stands on the spot where years ago stood an iron swing gate. This gate gave access to pathfields leading to Penlee, Beaumont House and Wingfield. Bluebells spread from the old cemetery to the fields where children picked buttercups and cows browsed!

This version of the book is virtually as originally published, presenting the work of Gerald W Barker. There are now additional pages at the back providing information about the publisher, Arthur L Clamp.

The republishing project is being managed by Arthur's grandson, Steven Gibson. We aim to find all the research that he was involved in publishing, preserving it for the next generation as part of 'The Clamp Collection'.

INTRODUCTION

"ROBERT FALCON SCOTT saddled his pony and leaving his house *Outlands* at Milehouse made his way past the thatched cottages opposite and surveyed the rural scene as he rode towards the iron swing gate, where the entrance to the bus depot is now. Having ridden across Penlee fields he would arrive at Exmouth House (later Exmouth Hall) having ridden along Somerset Place and Portland Road. Exmouth House was a private school which had long sheds at the rear (the length of what is now Milne Villas) for stabling the horses and ponies of the pupils." I challenge anyone who is interested in Devonport's history to listen to Mr. Arthur Rickard relating such accounts and not be fascinated by them.

At the rear of Kimber's (now Lang's) garage, in Albert Road, ran a long wooden staircase to Albert Road Halt. I often saw people hurrying down these stairs and along the railway track to take shelter in the tunnel, to the right of Exmouth Hall, when the air raid sirens sounded. Mr. and Mrs. Rickard remember leaving their house in Albert Road and standing in the recesses that existed every forty yards or so in the tunnel. On one occasion a train stopped in the tunnel during a raid so that lights from the engine flares would not give enemy bombers a sighting. The train's presence gave warmth and company to those taking shelter.

Talking to the men and women of Devonport has made my work on *Day's in Devonport* a worthwhile experience in itself. Mr. R. Smith, who was born in Mutton Cove, tells of a small recess outside the Dockyard South Gate in Fore Street where, at the time of the wooden ships, a gas jet stayed lit so that the Dockyard workers could light their cigarettes and pipes on leaving work as smoking inside was not allowed.

In the silent film era, Mr. Pat Ghillyer recalls how the cinemas, Tivoli, Electric and Hippodrome, became a second home for the poorer Devonport families. The children in the front of the Tivoli, sitting on the rows of hard wooden benches, had to gaze up hard to see the picture on the screen. There was only a pianist in those far off days and the kids used to cheer the roof off on Saturdays when she turned up to play for their matinee. It wasn't until 1928 that Harry Harcourt engaged a violinist and a man to play the cello. These remained until the advent of the "talkies". The *Tiv* opened up its first sound film with *His Glorious Night,* a Metro-Goldwyn-Mayor film starring the late John Gilbert. In the 1920s cups of tea were given out to the adults in the audience during the matinees.

I have had the pleasure of listening to many interesting stories about people and places of Devonport. Inside the Dockyard South Gate one would be met with the view of hundreds upon hundreds of cobble stones. "What's up Harry? Picking out the smooth ones?" would come the taunts from the fit Dockyard workers to a less fortunate colleague who had trouble with a foot or leg and found difficulty in walking to his place of work. Although the cobble stones went down to the official residences and down to the sea wall, there was an even path made between lines of trees for the ladies, to give them smooth access.

What became of the boys and girls of Geraldine Lamb dancers (Book II)? I had the pleasure of meeting one of them during his brief visit to Whitsands recently. Teddy Tout, the son of Geraldine Lamb, was the sergeant major in the Army Cadet Force Company of which I was a member. Now a Squadron Leader in the Royal Air Force he has been decorated with the M.B.E. for his work on bomb disposal.

I would like to thank the following for their help in the preparation of this third illustrated book on Devonport: Mr. A. Rickard, Mr. R. Smith, Mr. L. Bromley, Mr. A. Searle, Mrs. L. M. Hooper, Mrs. K. Mills, Geraldine Lamb (Sylvia and Valerie), Mr. P. F. Ghillyer, Mr. G. Sloggett, Mr. R. Burgoyne, Mr. J. Evans, Mr. M. Ware, Mr. R. Watkins, Mrs. J. Fitzpatrick and Mrs. P. Goad, Mr. R. Baser, Mr. A. Baser, Mr. H. Feabes.

My special thanks must go once again to Mr. Arthur L. Clamp who has encouraged me to record pre-war Devonport before memories fade for ever. He is one who is prepared to give up the most precious thing which is time. We spent a Sunday, for example, photographing many features of Devonport which may soon go for ever. A recent visit by him with a very large engraving showing the lines of fortifications around old Devonport in the 1860s means we are on the trail to a part IV in this series. Please keep looking for those old photographs!

Gerald W. Barker,
44 Burnham Park Road,
Peverell, Plymouth,
Telephone 784725
February, 1983

Appendix to Part II

Page 9: Two more names for the ladies wearing clogs. Mrs. Veitch in the back row, second from left, and her daughter, Florence, back row first left.

Page 10: The messenger boy is Ted Lillicrap who lived in Stoke village.

Page 20: The Royal Naval and Military Free Schools. Opened 1831 in King Street; 1902 transferred to Devonport Education Authority: 1941 destroyed by enemy action. 1929 should read 1919.

So This is Devonport

Jimmy James, well known for his manipulation of a cigarette when "drunk" on the stage, was in the revue, *So This is Devonport 1928-29*. The Hippodrome, later to become a cinema, had a sliding roof for ventilation during the interval. Mr. Pat Ghillyer, who remembers the projection room was in the roof, felt dizzy when he had helped to "open" the roof by using pulleys and then saw hundreds of faces far below looking up to the sky.

HIPPODROME
DEVONPORT
Phone — Dev. 109

A COUNTY CINEMA

Attractions for August

Commencing	Title	Featuring	Cert.
Mon. Aug. 7 6 days	Trouble Brewing	George Formby	U
	Swing Sister Swing	Johnny Downs	U
Mon. Aug. 14 6 days	Q Planes	Laurence Olivier Valerie Hobson Ralph Richardson	A
	Fighting Thoroughbreds	Mary Carlisle	U
Mon. Aug. 21 6 days	Stage Coach	John Wayne Claire Trevor	U
	Five of a kind	The Dionne Quins	U
Mon. Aug. 28 6 days	Idiot's Delight	Norma Shearer Clark Gable	A
	Magnificent Outcast	James Ellison	U

Continuous Performance Daily 2-0—10-30.

 Matinee Prices till 4 o'clock
Ground Floor 6d. Circle 1/-

Life Boat Inn, Fore Street

Mr. L. Bromley, aged 75 years, served as a barman here during the 1920s. He remembers the artists from the Hippodrome would frequent the inn. Among those he helped to serve was Gracie Fields who wore a grey seal-skin fur coat. The pub had a main bar, a bottle and jug, and lounge. In the doorway stands the publican, Mr. Banks, his barmaid, Nellie Boyle, and his daughter, Dolly Banks. In relation to the map of Fore Street (Part I) it is on the corner of St. Aubyn and Fore Street No. 105.

Saint Mary's School, 1922

A brisk walk from St. Paul's along King Street, Catherine Street and the cobble stones of James Street would bring one to Saint Mary's School. The boys' school was separate to the girls. The headmaster, Mr. Williams, is standing on the right. Mr. Martin, a teacher from Torpoint, is standing left. Alf Searle is second from the right front row. Other boys are: Jacky Ryan, Morris Albert Myers, Gibson and Mooney. The headmistress of the infants school was Miss Thorn.

St. Paul's Church

This church, badly damaged by enemy action and demolished by 1958, was situated in Morice Square opposite the Royal Fleet Club. St. Aubyn Church in 1959 incorporated St. Paul's, St. John the Baptist, St. Mary's and St. Stephens. The whole of old Devonport's thoroughfares were cobble-stoned, with the exception of Fore Street and Marlborough Street. They were the main thoroughfares and as such were the only two streets to have roadway surfaces of tarred wood blocks.

The Green Green Grass

Sailors of all nations would find resting on the grass of Devonport Park a luxurious alternative to their voyages at sea. The boys and girls in the 1930s were puzzled as to why so many men, three and four abreast and leading the length of the Dockyard wall from William Street to Marlborough Street, were slowly shuffling forwards down the hill. It was the time of much unemployment and the Labour Exchange was situated at the bottom of the hill.

Barrel Organ and Performing Monkey

Italians with the organ and monkey in Cumberland Street before 1914. Mr. E. B. Miles took grocery orders on Tuesday and delivered on Friday for Saint Budeaux. A less happy event took place on Tuesday, 30th August, 1842. "About nine o'clock nearly opposite Mr. Reed's the Hairdresser, Mr. Owen was struck a violent blow on the head. As this was the second assault on Mr. Owen in six days a £5 reward will be given for information that will bring the offender to justice".

Magnificent View

Even in the eighteenth century a magnificent view of Cremyll could be had. The small cottages on the right are in the vicinity of the present marina. Looking out to Barne Pool this view is taken approximately from the point where the path begins to Devonport Hill.

Camel's Head about 1910

The Devonport tram is passing West Ham Terrace. The shops advertise Reckitts Blue, Robin Starch and Goodbody's bread. In the wall opposite the inn could be read "2 miles to Plymouth". In 1835 the Rev. C. T. Collins-Trelawny, of Ham, erected the *Camel's Head Inn,* the first landlord being James Rickard. The wooden camel's head which was a part of the inn "disappeared" when the inn's name was changed to *The Submarine.*

George Street Carnival

The flags are out in 1954 (approx). The houses on the right hand side are now demolished and flats have been built. At the corner at the top right the well known Doctor Bradlaw had his surgery. His distinctive car horn during the 1930s could be heard when he sped past his patients' houses as far afield as Victoria Place in Stoke. His house was *Sungates,* the Spanish-style built building at Hartley.

The Queen's Tour

The Queen of Devonport Carnival 1933, Miss Laura Oldham, is leaving the Royal Albert Hospital, Devonport, after touring the wards. She is followed by her maids of honour: Dorothy Mandry, Eileen Barrett, Phyllis Bennie and Kathleen Ketteridge. The page, Miss Joan Marks in a mauve brocade suit and plumed hat, was bearing the crown on a purple velvet cushion.

Her majesty-elect wore a white satin gown girdled with gold and a long cloak of purple velvet trimmed with gold braid and embroidery and carrying a bouquet of mauve flowers tied with red and white ribbon, the hospital colours. Her cloak was borne by little Miss Betty Marks, who wore a white frock in mediaeval style with a flowing white net veil secured with a gold headband.

Thin Red Line

The red and white blazers of the well known Geraldine Lamb dancers who were always in the forefront of Devonport's helpers of good causes.

Royal Albert Hospital

The hospital for many years was supported entirely by voluntary contributions. The remains of a collecting box is still evident in the wall opposite the main entrance. Note the horse trough in Military Road that led to Granby Barracks. A skeleton could be seen at the top front window as one walked into Marlborough Street. On the left of the photo, now a car park, was a moat that was used as a shooting range.

Geraldine Lamb's Starlight Dancers

Principal of the Cobourg Street School of Dancing.

Opening Scene—7-15 to Dreamland	Company
Solo—Tap-a-tap	Gwendoline Randle
Sailor Scene	Starlights
Acrobatic Dance	Kathleen Powton (Winner of 7 Medals)
Duet—Song and Dance	Beryl Rattenbury and Pat Jane (Silver Cup and 2 Medals)
Swing your way to happiness	Pansy Hewitt and Starlets (Diploma)
Solo—Twinkle Feet	Sylvia Smith
Double Acrobatic Dance	Thelma Ferrit and Norma Serman (2 Silver Medals)
Solo—Tap Dance	Hellen Rowsell
Gypsy Scene	Starlights and Starlets
Song and Dance	Peggy Kennedy
The Dandies	Margaret Bullard and Sylvia Webb
12 Acrobatic Dancers	Starlight Wonders (Diploma)
Song and Dance	Betty Foster
Toe Tap	Margaret Gaylard
Pincushion Dance	6 Starlets
Speciality Dance	Diana Lane
Hawaiian Scene	Company
Solo Dance	Gladys Rowsell
Soldier and his Lady	Doreen Butt and Doreen Bradford
Acrobatic Dance	Daphne Foot
O Fie Pirroutte	3 Dancers
Song and Dance	Pat George
Military Ballet	Sylvia Webb
Tap Dance	Dennis Fryer
Ballet—Blue Danube.	Valerie Tout (Singer), Pansy Hewitt (Solo Dancer), and Company.

Geraldine Lamb

Geraldine Lamb, the Principal, had the early distinction of being born on Drake's Island. Her father was a soldier. She began in 1918 with her dancing school at Lambhay Hill. The family lived in the Barbican. The school of dancing continues under the leadership of Sylvia and Valerie Tout (the daughters of Geraldine Lamb and Teddy Tout, senior) in Connaught Avenue.

We're Going to get Lit Up!

8-11 p.m. Al Fresco Dance. Bandstand Enclosure. Admission 6d. Dance music by Lewarn and his Harmoniers M.C. Mr. A. Down. Young and old would enjoy dancing around the well lit bandstand. Electricity was brought from Tamar Terrace Tramway supply to light the bandstand in 1907. The circular enclosure was erected with an asphalt surface for concert parties, dancing, etc. Today the bandstand is gone but the enclosure remains.

Post-Blitz Messenger Boys

Boys between the ages of 14-18 years were formed into a special squad during the early 1940s to trace missing people after air raids. The headquarters was at the Citizens' Advice Bureau opposite the library in Tavistock Road. Devonport schoolboys in the photograph are Ivan Price, Alfred Rothery, Fred Merrin, Bill Massey and the author who also erected steel Morrison table air raid shelters in peoples' dining rooms or kitchens.

The Shopping Dormitory of the West

In happier times people would come from afar to shop in the numerous shops of Fore Street. During carnival weeks, "Spot the Error" would be featured in the shop windows. Tozers would have a nail in with its display of stockings, for example. The nissen huts were built during the war to be used as hospital wards for the wounded during the invasion. At the Y.M.C.A. concert in Aubyn Street servicemen could see Khuda Bux, *The Man With The X-Ray Eyes*.

Still Standing!

Marks and Spencer still remains but stripped of its former glory. The wall of the naval base now separates it from the Forum (one time cinema) in Fore Street. The street that once had those lovely Tiger-Leyland buses cruising full of servicemen and civilians, during the 1930s, was virtually destroyed in the Devonport blitz. Some cars had large rectangular gas bags on their roofs. Their engines were driven by gas, owing to fuel shortages.

College of Engineering erected 1879

Situated between Albert Road Dockyard Gate and St. Levan gate this large handsome building of Portland stone was the College for Royal Naval Engineering Officers before Manadon College (R.N.E.C.) was in use. Roman Catholic Officers and Midshipmen marched to and from the Roman Catholic Church at Mutton Cove, as there was no R.C. Church in the Royal Naval Barracks at one time.

What's That Doing Here Then?

These could have been the words of an irate sergeant major when he saw an army barracks with verandahs. The barrack building was earmarked for India but owing to a mix-up it was erected in Devonport. Raglan Barracks extended from Fore Street to Cumberland Road. The Royal coat of arms is in the pediment of the main archway built in 1853-6 by Captain Fowke.

St. Michael and St. Joseph

Roman Catholic soldiers would be marched to their garrison church at Mutton Cove, which was built in 1861 chiefly for the R.C. troops stationed in the Three Towns. Crowds would line the pavements in Pembroke Street to see the band leading the soldiers to the 09.30 mass. It was called the "Sunday Morning Spectacular" by the *Mercury* (forerunner of *Western Morning News*). Nearby the church stood *Sibley's Waggonettes*. They supplied lovely horses with shiny coats and superb coaches. They were as much a part of Old Devonport as the Statue of King Billy.

Two Towns
On the back of the Devonport and Stonehouse metal box was the inscription: J.S. Fry & Sons, Ltd. By appointment H.M. the King H.M. the Queen H.M. Queen Alexandra and other Royal Houses of Europe.

Devonport Market built 1852
The market, a handsome building in the italian style, with its tower at the south end being a fine specimen of an italian campanile, was, in the words of many people of Devonport "A joy to behold". It had a fish market and a meat market. Up the 8 feet wide staircase was the butter market where the butter pats were displayed. This market, with its clock tower, was a well known landmark and on market days Tuesdays, Thursdays and Saturdays, it took pride in that it drew shoppers from Plymouth, who flocked through the many entrances off Market Street, Duke Street, Catherine Street and, to the delight of children, Cumberland Street entrance where the toffee stall was the great attraction.

Sir John Jackson
He was a noted constructor in Devonport. Weston Mill was once known as *Sir John Jackson's estate*. He built it to house the workers at the Dockyard.

The Medal
It had a red, white and blue ribbon. Presented by Sir John and Lady Jackson Devonport. On the back: King George V and Mary. Crowned June, 1911.

Eyes Front!

The well known Alf Way is running a criticial eye over a section of the girls at drill. The Royal United Services Orphanage for Girls was at the top of Albert Road. It was erected in 1824 with wings added at later dates. This was an "asylum" for the female orphans of soldiers and sailors. It had its rear playground at Stoke Terrace. The orphanage was evacuated to Newquay in 1940. The building, now a Government Office, stands today a tribute to the builders and craftsmen of the past. The building was occupied by Polish sailors during the war.

St. Michael's Church

A view of the "railway cut" that ran from Exmouth Road to Havelock Terrace where the Church Hall now stands. It was at one time a muddy swamp. It was erected in 1843 and consecrated 1845 with 1,200 sittings, many of which were free, during the time of the Rev. R. Gardner, who resided in Navy Row, now Albert Road. During the war the Vicar's home guard boots and gaiters below his cassock were visible to the choir boys as he gave his sermon.

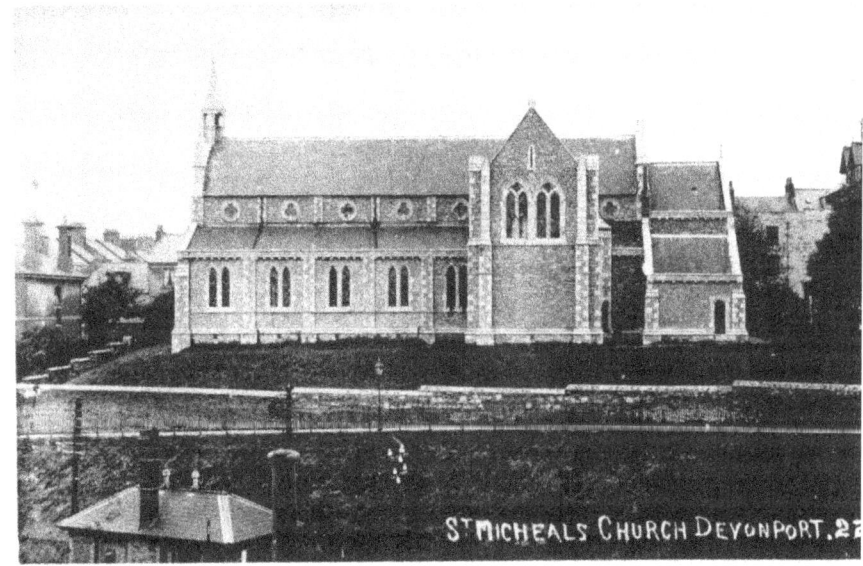

Devonport Royal Dockyard Orphanage

Situated near the Milehouse traffic lights, it was the third building to be used as a Dockyard Orphanage. The previous two were old houses of the gentry in Morice Square. Rockey's Farm, seen on the left, had a huge cobble stone yard where horses were "broken in". The hedge and enclosing farm and fields ran along to the swing gate in Alma Road.

Milne Place

A railway line was to be built along the flat part of the park opposite Milne Place. It was to run from Albert Road Station to the Torpoint Ferry. It never materialised, although the map of Devonport, 1860, clearly shows the line. During the war an American soldier, sitting just above the public air raid shelter (where the proposed railway line was to have been built), said to some Morice Town boys, as he surveyed the numerous blitzed houses "Hell! I thought this was all propaganda back in the States."

Alcester Street

The street was built in 1887. The view today from this spot almost the same as the view taken around 1904 despite the many Dockyard extensions. The spire of Saint James the Great Church has vanished along with the church which was demolished in 1959 with the merger plans. Situated in Keyham Road, the Church was badly damaged in the raids 1939-45. If any boy or girl pupil of Saint James the Great School was still in the vicinity of Alcester Street when the school bell rang for registration they had to run like greyhounds.

Pentamar Terrace

Vegetables were grown in every available spot along the top of the railway bank. Boys making an escape from the rival Pym Street, Garden or John Street gangs, would hastily climb over the railing near the wall and running along the bank overlooking the railway track would make their way to safety by climbing over the wall of the railway bridge in Haddington Road.; Pentamar Terrace was destroyed by enemy action, when a land-mine caused great destruction on 17th May, 1941.

Charlotte Street, Devonport

A walk past the slate hung houses of Charlotte Street and hair stylist would bring one to Albert Road. Across this road would be the scnool clinic and Morice Town School. In Charlotte Street was held one of the many victory street parties after the Second World War. Sailors walking up Albert Road joined in the celebrations when they saw the dancing.

Penlee Gardens, Stoke

Stoke has many fine buildings such as these here. Not far away is Cundy's horse and carts which were kept in stables in the grounds of the present Penlee Secondary School. In the same area a German plane had crashed after being shot down. It was one of the everyday sights in the war for boys walking along the narrow path leading to Alma Road.

Haddington Road

Not far up the hill from the regal-looking houses is the Blockhouse, with one of the finest views in the city. Walking down towards Charlotte Street one would see the Methodist Chapel on the left. Boys and girls in the 1930s would enjoy going to the Band of Hope and seeing slides on the magic lantern. Houses on the right, opposite the Chapel, were badly damaged in 1941 and have now given place to a new Salvation Army Hall.

BOYHOOD MEMORIES OF DEVONPORT

Roger Watkins

King Street Naval and Military School

I attended this school from 1921 and remember the headmaster of the senior school for boys being a Mr. Steed, a martinet and not very popular with the pupils. Mr. Chandler was the deputy head. Mr. Atwell taught some boys to play the violin after school hours at 6d. a lesson. There was also Mr. Wood, Mr. Drake, Mr. James and Mr. Stone. As the years pass one remembers more vividly the good things but for myself I think King Street School was a very happy one with an excellent teaching staff who were respected and helpful but stood no nonsense.

All the pupils of my time had to remember multiplication tables which were repeated almost like songs and heard throughout the Junior School. This repetition made its mark as the majority of boys were good at tables. Penmanship was repeatedly practised with a "J" type nib ink pen, the writing was legible and in many cases beautifully written.

Various Pastimes and Leisures

A game of marbles was a great favourite in Jessamine Place until a shout was heard "Wakey" boys. This call was generally inevitable and was a sign for everyone to grab their marbles including the older boys who had made the foregoing shout. During the winter the school was opened for certain evenings, including holidays, as a play centre with one or two teachers in attendance. The evening was occupied with raffia work, painting, drawing, draughts, ludo and table tennis then called "ping pong".

Outside of the play centre a game in the streets called *Jack, Jack, show your light*, was played with the aid of a torch being flicked off and on enabling that boy to be observed and caught. Another game was *Relieve O*. For light evenings we had steel hoops propelled with a steel crook but unfortunately after considerable usage and hitting curbs when guiding the hoop onto the pavement, it would break resulting in a visit to the blacksmith to have the ends welded together at a cost of 1d.

Saturday afternoons could be a great treat visiting a local cinema. There was Camel's Head picture house which later became a police sub-station, the picture house in William Street, Morice Town, Ford *Palladium* in St. Levan's Road and the *Tivoli* at the top end of Fore Street. Here a certain number of the earliest arrivals who had to line up in the fire escape lane adjoining the building received an orange or apple or a comic, such as *Funny Wonder, Comic Cuts, Tiger Tim* or *Rainbow*. I expect many people remember at Aggie Westons there used to be a short service during the winter on Wednesday evenings after which a screen was raised on the platform and films were shown for about one and a half hours. A collection was taken on going out.

My favourite picture house was the *Tivoli* and the serials. If my memory serves me right they were of Eddy Polo as *Elmo the Mighty*, the Tarzan serials, Pearl White, Rin Tin Tin and many others. I remember the piano in the corner which was later augmented with a violin and was it a cello? There was also the *Electric* but as yet the *Hippodrome* and *Alhambra* were still variety theatres.

We youngsters in Devonport must remember the tram terminus near the Naval Fleet Club and St. Paul's Church sadly destroyed in the raids of April, 1941. There were double lines on New Passage Hill and going through the process of changing lines it has been known for the brake shoes to slip resulting in the tram travelling about fifteen to twenty yards towards the club and crashing. Actually I saw a man on the top deck vault over the top rails when this happened. He sustained injuries and was taken to the Royal Albert Hospital, renamed the Devonport Hospital.

Writing about this incident reminded me how youngsters were admitted to hospital to have their tonsils removed. Each one, accompanied by an adult, had to find their way to the hospital and sit with others in a waiting room near the operating theatre. Perhaps there were three or four to be done and eventually a nurse would call for one of the patients who was led away lowering our spirits somewhat. After about thirty minutes the nurse returned carrying the unconscious youngster and laying him out on a couch then calling for the next patient. Meanwhile the first boy had started to recover with blood smeared around his mouth, perhaps spattered on cheeks, all of which we had to observe which was rather depressing to say the least. Eventually all the boys had their tonsils removed and recovered enough to leave and find their own way home with a parent. Their heads and throats were swathed in bandages and naturally they were not feeling too good. Others living further away had to catch a tram from near the hospital.

Living near an army barracks, a park, the Dockyard and the open sea enlivened our pleasures enormously and having friends living in the Granby Barracks, holding perhaps a battalion of men with many horses, gave two or three of us golden opportunities to enter this military establishment. It was sited at the east end of the Devonport hospital and we took risks. There were hay ricks to jump up and explore, horses to watch and always a visit to the cookhouse where, if the cook was in a good mood, he had only to be asked and a pocket of hard tack biscuits wrapped in grease proof paper was handed to each one of us with great relish. Leaving the barracks we would stop and watch the farrier at work whose workshop was situated outside the main gates. An hour could easily be whiled away here.

We would then visit the park to see the grazing sheep, the entrance up the steps leading from New Passage Hill. Our intention was to walk across the path leading to the steps at the top of Ferry Road and the whole area was a separate field with railings around with the ground sloping towards New Passage Hill where shrubs were grown. The sheep grazed for a week or two until required to be driven to the private Devonport market butchers' abbatoir.

The Dockyard hooter had sounded signifying the end of the day for the workers and several would go to a recess in the wall in which there was a lighted gas jet. Here they would get their pipes or cigarettes lit as smoking in the yard was not allowed from 9 a.m. to 11 a.m. and 2.0 p.m. to 3.30 p.m. and only in workshops where braziers, fire hearth torches for welding purposes, were in use. The wall jets were fitted close to all the main gates.

We often visited Sparrow Park next to the Dockyard fire engine house and facing Albert Road then jumped over the railings into Tamar Road, walked through Moon Street and stopped outside the police sub-station near the Labour Exchange in Ferry Road. We would wait for the police to man the station who had signed the duty attendance register to leave and be inspected. Six or seven policemen lined up for inspection by the duty sergeant their capes slung over their right shoulders and tucked into a leather belt. On the left of this was fixed a black rectangular paraffin lamp. I cannot recall from this time, 1923, them having electric torches. The police turned right and marched off up New Passage Hill in single file. On reaching Marlborough Street the last man would detach himself and go to his beat as did the rest of them in turn.

The Lean Years between 1920 and 1930

It was a common sight to see youngsters waiting for men to leave the Dockyard at the end of the day and asking them, "Any lefts, Sir?" whereon the man asked may have produced from his bag a sandwich or a couple of biscuits for the lad. At this time poverty was rife as a result of the Great War but thank goodness things improved towards the end of the 1920s. Soup kitchens had been set up at various points in the town and about a pint of soup could be had for 2d. Money was very scarce; there were innumerable one-parent families due to the father being killed in the war and also many men returned unable to work due to injuries or lack of jobs.

Stonehouse Creek

Then there was Stonehouse Creek commonly called *Tinkies*, a tidal creek in which Fox and Elliot rafted a large number of various kinds of timber logs to season which were anything up to 50 feet long and about 18 inches by 18 inches in section down to 12 inches by 12 inches all chained together. When needed logs were released and pulled by motor boat to the sawmill. We boys used to swim in the creek and run along the logs but sometimes on an incoming tide this could be dangerous as it would pull a youngster under a log.

At eight or nine years of age some fun could be had by jumping and sitting on the back axle of a hansom cab or a four-wheeled brougham but sometimes the driver's whip flicked over the top of the vehicle to our astonishment. We were a little naive and it never crossed our minds that the driver would look into a shop window and see us in the reflections.

The anecdotes referring to Mr. Blagdon and Mr. Fletcher reminded me of the times we went to the pigeon loft of one of them. Pigeons were a great hobby and although there were several racing Pigeon clubs a large number of boys kept their own birds and took them to various places to release them. This gave us much satisfaction.

Pocket Money

Obviously money was in short supply in my early days but many boys managed to do some jobs which brought in a few coppers to spend. A penny could buy quite a lot with boiled sweets at 1½d. a quarter and treacle toffee at a 1d. for two ounces. Jaffa oranges were seven for 6d., one pasty at Stephens and Risdons, with plenty of meat, for 2d. so providing money was available food on the whole was quite reasonable.

A favourite job was to await the arrival of trains at the Devonport, G.W.R. and Devonport L. and S.R. stations and then offer to show passengers to the trams or carry their baggage for 1d. or even 2d. Other boys found Saturday jobs helping in various kinds of shops especially those selling fruit. Windows had to be washed, pavements cleaned down and swept and entrances to the shop itself cleared and placing goods in order were all part of the day's work. An excellent job was always being an assistant to the driver of the baker's van. It was long hours and very busy but enjoyable. The boy reported at the bakery at 7 a.m. by which time the driver had already harnessed his horse to the van and was waiting outside the bakery entrance with the van floor covered in clean flour sacking. The man and boy loaded it with various kinds of loaves, some 1 lb., others 2lb. which by law had to be the minimum after baking. This was at Stephens and Risdons and the shop and bakery extended from Marlborough Street through Albany Lane to Morice Street. Away we went, stopped at noon for dinner of shop pasties then returning for another load of bread for the afternoon's delivery which finished around 4.30 p.m. The van was emptied and cleaned out while the driver took the money and cash book into the shop. The driver and boy then drove to the stables in Granby Lane, unharnessed the horse, wiped him down and then gave him a bag of oats and a good drink of water. The horse was bedded down with clean straw and hay placed in the feeding grill. On returning to the shop the boy received his wages and a bag of buns to take home.

On the River

The coal burning propellor-driven steamer plying from Torpoint across to North Corner and onto Pottery Quay was popular with the boys of my years. The round trip took about three quarters of an hour and cost 1d. The boat was built on the lines of the Cremyll steamer but I think slightly smaller. To have a trip for 1d. was marvellous. The steamer was named *Lady Beatrice* after a well known notability at Torpoint.

There was also the paddle steamer *Britannia* which did the trip to Millbrook for passengers to walk or travel by wagonette on to Whitsands. The trip cost 6d. each way. I remember how disappointed everyone was if the tide was at low ebb when going to Millbrook and we then had to land at South Down or Anderton. This was a disaster for us lads when returning from Whitsands as it meant we had to walk the extra distance from Millbrook.

Some rowing boat photographs have been produced in book two in this series and it is very sad that the days of these clubs have gone due, I suppose, to the high cost of replacing boats no longer fit for service. Cutters of 26 feet and whalers of 27 feet were obtained from the naval stores department in the Dockyard and bought at auction. We then had a large Navy and many of these boats went to auction as they became too costly to maintain. A club was lucky in getting one of these boats and had plenty of young men to put them into good working order. Just about every church club, including the Y.M.C.A., and the Royal Engineering College at Keyham had one or two boats and on Saturdays the various clubs could be seen going out of the Hamoaze into the Sound. If the tide was rising they would make their way up the Tamar. Rowing was a great hobby especially in an organised rowing club.

Old names for Local Places

During the 1930s many young men would spend an evening perhaps in Torpoint or Saltash. When speaking of Torpoint the name used was Typhee a popular word which was used in the first line of a song We are the boys of the old Typhee! etc. also when speaking of Saltash the name used was Tywops and it was most common to hear these names used in the Mutton Cove vicinity where I used to live.

15

M^r^s James Ware.

In a/c with

The Capital and Counties Bank, Limited

Estab^d 1834. DEVONPORT.

Dr   Cr

THE Largest, Cheapest and most up-to-date Drapery and Furnishing Stores in the West of England. The Latest addition to our Establishment is the opening of our New Furniture Arcade which is being largely patronised. Our New Millinery Saloons in Tavistock Street and adjoining our Main Premises, are replete with the very latest styles in French and English Modes, and the abilities of a Competent Milliner and large staff will be found equal to any demand which may be made on them. Special attention to Post Orders. Carriage Paid per Rail and Steamer on Goods to the value of £1 and upwards. **Catalogues free on application.** Visitors to Devonport and District will find this the most comprehensive and in every way satisfactory emporium in which to make their purchases.

Note addresses: **H.J. & E.A. BOOLDS Ltd.,** Adjoining the Market 1, 2, 3, 4, 5, 6, 7, 8, 31, 32, 33, Market St., Tavistock St., Sydney St. & Cross St. DEVONPORT.

Boold's Large Shop

Many Devonport people have spoken of their memories of this shop that was as well known as *Tozers*. Mrs. Marjorie Laxton remembers the Michelin-type figure in their window that was inflated and moved up and down. His name was *Billy-By-Bendum* and he was a great attraction.

Devonport Group Overseas

Not far across the sea, in fact, at Whitsands in Cornwall, a favourite spot to "get away from it all". John Evans, who is on the extreme right, later worked as a decorator in the Alhambra. He remembers the fire officer and police checking seats, etc., when changing from being the Metropole, 1924. Patrons in the orchestra stalls had to have their own toilets, so Wallie Rice, the proprietor, had to arrange to have drains connected to the new conveniences in Catherine Street. Others in the photograph are: Mr. and Mrs. Bailey, Harry and Eddie Bailey.

National Aluminium Week, 1932

Ralph and Son was a well known shop in Stoke village. It stood on the left hand side going towards Albert Road. The owner also, at one time, owned the *Stoke Inn*. In the mews was a blacksmith who shoed many horses at his anvil.

Stoke Public School

The school occupied the premises of the present Stoke Damerel High School for Girls. The playground was on the roof of the building. This tall structure could be seen from far afield. Pre-war there were few high buildings and very few with flat roofs. The top of this building held a fascination for many youngsters.

Royal Katie

Katie is the constant companion of two Devonport women. Mrs. Lilian Hooper, who has long been a champion of Devonport's heritage, is 80 years old and her companion Mrs. Goad, a well known nurse and health visitor to Devonport schools in the 1930s, is the dog's owner. Since a visit of Prince Charles, when the dog received a pat on the head, the two women of George Street insist on the prefix "Royal" for their pet.

St. Mary's (Devonport) Parish Church Choir, August, 1949

Back row:- Mr. C. Forrest, Mr. R. Taylor, Mr. C. May, Mr. D. Taylor, Mr. McLean, W. Evans, J. Brain, A. McLean, J. Cadd, T. Golden and T. Cotter. *Middle row:* D. Hillier, D. Evans, R. Brain, P. Travers, J. Golden, B. Mann, D. Taylor, R. Cadd and D. Read. *Front row:* Mr. D. Chubb, Mr. H. Gendle, W. Stafford, Mr. V. W. Kercher, *Lay Reader,* Rev. G. A. Bennett, M.A., *Vicar,* Mr. R. A. C. Wilkins, *Organist and Choirmaster,* P. Boundy and Mr. N. Crocker.

The Mayor & Mayoress of Devonport

(*Mr. E. Blackall*)   (*Mrs. J. G. Greaves*)

send Christmas Greetings

and all

Good Wishes for the New Year.

Guildhall,
Devonport,
Xmas, 1913.

DEVONPORT.

Created, 13th October, 1837. Extended, 12th August, 1898.

Members of Parliament.—Sir John Jackson, 48, Belgrave Square, London, S.W
Sir C. Kinloch Cooke, 3, Mount Street, Grosvenor Square, London, W.

Mayor.—EDWARD BLACKALL, Esq.

Recorder.—H. E. Duke, Esq., K.C., M.P.

Borough Magistrates.—W. Banister, E. Blackall, G. Breeze, J. F. F. Cole, M. Fredman, P. C. Goodman, H. J. H. Graves, A. W. Grigg, J. Heard, W. Hornbrook, Sir John Jackson, B. James, H. Jarvis, J. Jolliffe, E. M Leest, W. Littleton, J. B. Love, R. D. Monk, W. J. Moon, W. H Mountstephen, W. H. Pote, G. A. Rae, A. J. Rider, G. Risdon, W. H Roberts, G. T. Rolston, E. St. Aubyn, R. Smerdon, G. H. Smith, A Stephens, J. C. Tozer, W. J. Waycott, and H. Williams.

Aldermen.—Edward Blackall, William Cousins, James Day, Myer Fredman, Thomas Husband Gill, John Philip Goldsmith, William Hornbrook, Henry Jarvis, James Joliffe, Edgar May Leest, William Littleton, Joseph Boyd Love, George Thomas Risdon, James Clarke Tozer, William John Waycott

Councillors (45)—

Morice Ward—John Mayne, Frederick A. Screech, John A. B. Weeks

Princes Ward—Charles Frederick Hocking, John William May (one vacancy, election pending at time of printing).

St. Aubyn Ward—Edwin Birch, John A. M. Heard (one vacancy, election pending at date of printing).

St. John's Ward—George Richard Archer, Israel Fredman, Samuel Allen Perkins

Clowance Ward—Thomas Ash Clarke, Alfred Goodman (one vacancy, election pending at time of printing).

Tamar Ward—Richard John Chappell, John Hellen, Walter R. Littleton

Clarence Ward—J. T. Jane, Alfred G. Phillips, William Henry Watson

Keyham Ward—William Jenkin, John Moon, William John Olver

Ford Ward—John James Hamlyn Moses, William H. Roberts, Percy Douglas Martin Rudall

Molesworth Ward—Fred Robert Charlick, Reginald McDonald, William Henry Welsford

Nelson Ward—John James Cramer, Thomas P. Treglohan, Andrew Weakford

Stoke Ward—James Francis Faulkener Cole, William Samuel May, Frederick Viggers

Pennycross Ward—Thomas Doney, William George, Walter John Smith

Station Ward (St. Budeaux)—Thomas George Essenhigh, William Henry Jackson, James Ware

Tamerton Ward—Fredk. D. Baxter, George A. Daymond, Richard Tozer

Borough Officers.—*Town Clerk, Clerk to the Urban Sanitary Authority*, R. J. Fittall *Deputy Town Clerk*, E. Rupert Royle. *Clerk of Peace*, R. J. Fittall *Clerk to the Borough Magistrates*, Foster J. Bone. *Borough Treasurer*, H J. Hoare *Medical Officer of Health*, O. Hall. *Public Analyst*, T. Tickle. *Borough Surveyor*, John F. Burns. *Gas Engineer*, W. P. Tervet. *Surgeon of the Police Force*, T. McElwaine. *Superintendent of Police*, J. H. Watson. *Borough Librarian* W. D. Rutter. *Coroner*, James A. Pearce. *Inspector of Weights and Measures* Edwin R. Collings. *Collectors of Rates*, W. Williams, James W. Harris F. Alford, T. G. Horlford, W. Bryant, R. Roberts. *Electrical Engineer*, James Walter Spark. *Water Engineer*, F. W. Lillicrap. *Director of Education*, W. H Crang. *Mayor's Auditor*, John Mayne. *Elective Auditors*, A. W. C. Stanbury C. Taylor. *Chief Inspector under the Diseases of Animals Act, 1894*, J. H. Watson *Inspector of Nuisances and under the Sale of Food and Drugs Acts* J. Thorning *Superintendent of Cleansing Department*, Walter Arscott.

— 1912. —

Devonport Corporation

Remembrancer

From December 16th

To December 23rd.

Swiss & Co., Fore St., Devonport.

Monday, December 23rd.

Hospital Visitors for week, Messrs. Rendle and Roberts.

Gas - - - 10-30 a.m.
(Aldermen Cousins and
  Jarvis - - 10-15 a.m.

Water - - 11-30 a.m.
(Alderman Fredman 11-15 a.m.)

Education (at the
  Education Office.) 3-0 p.m.

A Lovely Market Clock Tower

A view of Fore Street, Morice Street, King Street and Queen Street with the Dockyard wall on the extreme left. Centre foreground are the remains of Cherry Garden Street School (later York Street School) and Devonport Market Tower. The little dark new road on the left is roughly where Catherine Street was.

Spot the Twins

A photograph taken at King Street Council School 1927-28 in the playground. The twins, born during the Great War, were named Dorothy Somme Baser and Vera Verdun Baser. They are standing in the back row. Other girls were; Emma White and Lola Dean. The Headmistress was Miss Cole.

Reg and Arthur Baser, who were pupils in the Boys' section of the school in 1922, remember that violin lessons were available. On the payment of sixpence a week the few pupils that could afford to pay for lessons and violin by instalments, had Miss Mary Atwell to teach them.

Alpine Echoes

A lone trumpeter would stand on the top of the column (civilians had to pay 2d. for the privilege). He would play the required echo to a piece of music called *Alpine Echoes*. The military bands often played inside Devonport's Guildhall which was and still is a noble and handsome edifice designed after the style of the Parthenon at Athens and completed in 1822. Mr. Pat Ghillyer remembers the music resounding around the four magnificent columns and through the windows of the Guildhall that had been left open for all to hear.

Military Hospital

All "sick and hurt" were brought by water. The *Nightingale* and later the *Cavell* were the boats used each day and night with very little ceremony and the more fortunate survived. Later the hospital became schools, and at present are occupied by Devonport High School for Boys and Tamar High. The area between the hospital and Stonehouse bridge was known as *Tinkies* and numerous bulks of wood floated in Deadlake.

South Western Railway

A funeral procession passing through Paradise Road when ten victims of the A8 submarine disaster were interred at the Plymouth cemetery on 15th June, 1905. In the left foreground is the London and S.W. Railway. The College of Further Education now stands on this site. The platforms of this station were constructed of a length beyond the normal. This was to facilitate the arrival of troop trains. Raglan Barracks is not very far away. It was from this station that weary French soldiers marched to the barracks after Dunkirk in 1940.

Wilton Street

Note the high destination boards and the open air treatment for crew and passengers. This street has witnessed many processions. At the end of the war in Europe the Victory Parade made its way past Stoke Damerel Church with the military bands and servicemen of the Allies marching towards Albert Road.

Miss Agnes Weston
At the Royal Naval Barracks in 1899 Miss Agnes Weston talks to those she cared so much about — sailors of the Royal Navy. The rapid rise after the 1914—1918 war of N.A.A.F.I. made little impact on *Aggies* but bombs of the 1939 war removed for all time Devonporet's largest single building.

The Royal Sailors' Rest
Part of the Russian crew of the cruiser *Cesarevitch* at a reception in *Aggies* early in 1909. The Sailors' Rest was also used for such meetings as the *Penny in the Pound Hospital Scheme*. A room could be rented and on Sundays concerts were held. Mr. P. Ghillyer remembers the huge doorman who looked like an ex-Guardsman with his row of medals. On Thursday evenings the main hall was open to all the children of Devonport to "see the pictures". No matter which children caused trouble the doorman made a bee-line for the Cornwall Street kids to chuck 'em out first.

Admiralty House, Devonport.

Admiralty House, Devonport
Built in 1795, it was for 140 years the home of the Port Admiral. In 1934 the C-in-Chief moved over to Government House. A huge nineteen hundredweight brass bell found in a disused Chinese temple was brought home to Devonport for Sir Edward Seymour in 1902 on the cruiser *Pique*.

Johnstone Terrace, Keyham
See the "sun hats" on the milk churns and the taps poking out through the tail board. On the opposite side of the road the pavement would be full of people during Navy Week queueing up to make their way into the Royal Naval Barracks during the 1930s.

Quicksilver
The famous Devonport stage coach *Quicksilver* completed the Fore Street Gate run to London in twenty-one and a quarter hours during the early decades of the last century.

Here We Go!
Many trams would be seen "catching their breath" in Fore Street, having previously stormed St. Aubyn Street, before proceeding down Chapel Street and through the halfpenny gate, after passing the Post Office, Mount Stephens, *The Brown Bear*, Guardians' Relief, Manor Office and St. Aubyn Church. Here a no. 12 is on its lengthy run to Prince Rock. When buses began to slowly replace the trams, locals called them *Yellow Perils*.

Arthur L. Clamp – the man behind the books

Arthur Leslie Clamp was a man of boundless energy with a passion for helping others, particularly through his love of history. A printer by trade, he started his career in a printing company before moving his family from Exeter to Plymouth to teach at the Plymouth College of Art and Design, where he eventually became the Head of the Printing Department.

Arthur with his five children.

A Devoted Family Man

Despite his love of teaching, Arthur prioritised his family, always making it home by 5:30pm for tea. He and his wife, Rosemary, raised five children: Susan, Angela, Elizabeth, David, and Steven. Arthur would often combine his love of family and history by taking his children on Sunday walks, encouraging them to appreciate historical monuments by taking photos or making crayon rubbings of gravestones for his books. The family home at 203 Elburton Road was a hub of activity, with a large garden, featuring a two-storey fort and a makeshift swimming pool.

A Lifelong Learner and Adventurer

Arthur's thirst for knowledge extended beyond history to a deep curiosity about the world. He was passionate about exploring different cultures, traditions, and cuisines, often taking advantage of his long summer holidays as a teacher to travel to places like India, Russia, South America, the middle east and the USA, sometimes bringing one of his children along. This adventurous spirit even influenced his home life, as seen by the short-lived family tradition of steam-cooking vegetables after a trip to Iceland.

History is a prominent feature of family days out

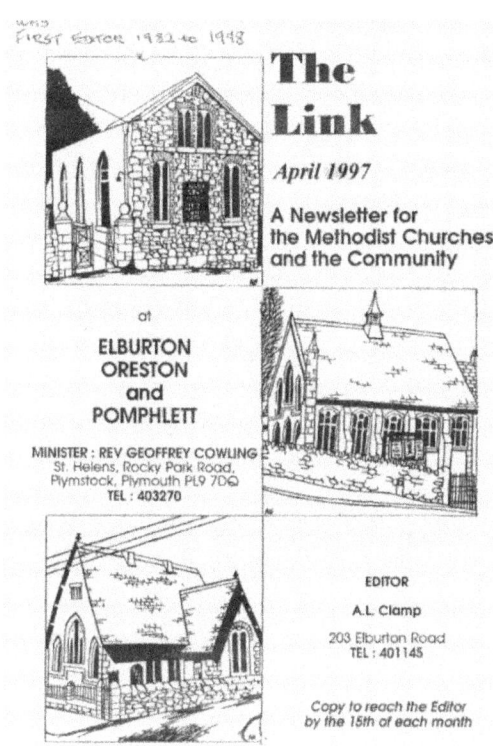

Community and Philanthropic Spirit

His commitment to serving others was evident in his long-standing involvement with the Elburton Methodist Church. He was the Sunday School Superintendent for over 15 years and served as the editor of the wider church's monthly newsletter, "The Link," for a similar duration. After Rosemary's very sad passing, Arthur later remarried and, following a chance encounter with a professor from India, established a connection with a missionary school in Chennai. Together with his new wife, Christine, he co-founded a "Sponsor a Child's Education" program that continues to this day.

*Pictured left – The cover of 'The Link' complete
with hand drawn sketches of each church by Angela
Below right – Arthur Clamp promoting his latest book
Below left – Arthur at home with his first wife, Rosemary
Below centre – Arthur on holiday with his second wife,
Christine*

A Legacy of Learning and Positivity

Arthur's greatest passion was history, which he brought to life through tireless research, documentation, and the many books he authored. He was driven by a need to "never be stuck in a rut," constantly seeking new experiences, meeting new people, and expanding his knowledge. With a positive attitude and a great sense of humour, he was always ready to help others, leaving a lasting impact on his family and community. His children, Susan, Angela, Elizabeth, David, and Steven, remember him with love and gratitude.

David Clamp, 2025

A Legacy of Local History

Below is the story of how Arthur L Clamp began writing books, in his own words, drafted shortly before he passed away in 2001. I have only made minor alterations to this text, correcting grammatical errors that he did not survive to correct himself. When I first discovered this text, I was shocked to see my name mentioned. It seems that, unbeknownst to me, I shared my first PC with him. I suspect he used it during the day when I was at school, although I do have one memory of sitting with him and showing him how it worked. It has been a pleasure to pick up where he left off and see his books republished and redistributed, and to know that I was part of the story, even back then. It was also fascinating to discover that his pricing structure matches the way I have tried to price the books, with a third going to local sellers and the rest covering printing costs with a little left over for my expenses.

I am his eldest grandson, and it is a privilege to curate his legacy, which we are calling 'The Clamp Collection'. The very last line of the text originally reads "The following pages list all the titles." Sadly, that page is missing and we have no record of all the books he published and knowing that some of those were researched by other authors makes the process of finding them even harder. I look forward to one day completing the collection and seeing them all available again. And maybe, one day, I'll even start writing my own to add to the series. For now, here is his story in his own words.

Steven Gibson, 2025

Writing and Publishing Booklets on Local Topics and Areas

I started this interest in either 1968 or 1969 when living in Woodford. I had by these dates established the Department of Printing and I think I must have been looking for something different to do. The first titles were of A5 size proofed from type set at Clarke, Doble and Brendon, Ltd., Plymouth printers, and then made up into pages and printed at Sawtell and Neilson, Ltd., Totnes.

Then began a slow process of getting them out to shops, etc. which proved to be more time consuming and difficult than actually researching, writing and getting the books into print. However, I persisted and opened a business account with Barclays Bank on the Broadway. I was advised to give it a title so I called it "Westway Publications". There came along another problem, one of storage of paper and finished books which was solved when the family moved to Elburton in 1970.

I changed the printer to Penwell, Ltd., Callington, Cornwall, as he was then just setting up himself and his prices seemed very reasonable. I did not get any of the printers to make up the complete books. I hand folded the flat printed sheets, stitched the books on a small manual table stitcher and trimmed them in a small hand turned guillotine which I bought from someone in Penzance for £40. It was brought up in a van.

The trouble and time going to and fro to Callington was too much so I transferred the printing to PDS Printers, Prince Rock, Plymouth, and I have been with them ever since. Now they are at Plympton which is easy to reach and they fold the flat sheets which was turning out to be a long chore which only saved a small part of the printing costs.

All my first titles were written by myself. I took the photographs and developed them in the loft of the house, the type was set by now on a computer situated in the house at Elburton from which I had collected photographic lengths of text to cut up and law down as pages.

At some point I decided that I would do my own film processing of lith film so I bought a large second hand process camera from Kingsbridge and learnt through trial and error to make line negatives of the text and halftone negatives of the illustrations which proved more difficult than I anticipated. The main problem was trying to keep the developer in the large dish at the correct temperature as any change would affect the developing time. I replaced this old camera with a brand new one bought from Croydon, Surrey, costing £900. This has turned out to be a great asset cutting out an expensive part of the printer's costs and one crucial aspect of the work which I could control.

By the middle 1970s there were many outlets I had contacted in Plymouth, up to Dartmoor, Exeter, around to Torbay, Totnes, Dartmouth and the South Hams. The market for local books was much greater than I had first thought and through getting to know many local people undertaking research themselves had the chance to help and make up books for other people who had in most instances, got together a collection of photographs with some text in a rather muddled way. Through my experience in print I was able to shape up their work and get it into print and in every case I had to pay the printer and let the person have the royalties. In the majority of titles produced in this manner this was another way of producing titles and it did give some profit to my work. However, I must say that in a few cases I lost out by either the other person getting the numbers wrong, not returning any monies from stock I delivered or they thought that more of their books should have been sold.

The print run was usually 1,000 copies and from time to time I have had reprints of 250 copies. It took about ten years to clear the first print run so I always had large stocks in the garage, workshop, etc. The numbers sold during the early years was about 7,000 copies a year increasing to around 9,000 copies and for the whole of the enterprise about 500,000 have been sold. The booklets have become part of the local scene and many people collect them, shops regularly order copies and I go around certain areas month by month restocking or replacing titles as necessary.

During the past year or so I have started setting the text on a Packard Bell PC, something which I should have done some years back. I share it with Steven Gibson, my grandson. There appears to be no end to the market for local books, but I could not earn a regular income because of the long time it takes to sell stock.

However, now exceeding 100 titles made up mainly of A4 twenty-four page booklets, some folded guides, with selling prices set with a third going to the shop which is the trade custom, the original idea has been quite successful and could go on for ever.

Apart from monetary benefits, however spasmodically these might be, I have learnt a lot myself, met many interesting people and have become part of the local scene with requests to give talks and to advise people about getting into print.

Arthur L Clamp, 2001

This newspaper article, published by the Evening Herald on 17th August 2001, forms a good record of his life. Just as he encourages us to learn more about local history, we encourage you to learn a little about him. For that reason, we have included these pages at the back of all the most recently republished books, in honour of his memory and recognition of his contribution to the community.

www.ingramcontent.com/pod-product-compliance
Lightning Source LLC
Chambersburg PA
CBHW061407070526
44584CB00031B/4178